#THIS IS #WHAT ANXIETY FEELS LIKE

WHEN YOU THINK EVERYONE HATES YOU & SO MUCH MORE

SARAH FADER
MICHELLE HAMMER

board

TO ALL THE ANXIOUS PEOPLE WHO THINK EVERYONE HATES THEM.
#ThisIsWhatAnxietyFeelsLike

I'M SO OVERWHELMED BY THE AMOUNT OF WORK I HAVE TO DO, THAT I CAN'T GET STARTED.

#ThisIsWhatAnxietyFeelsLike

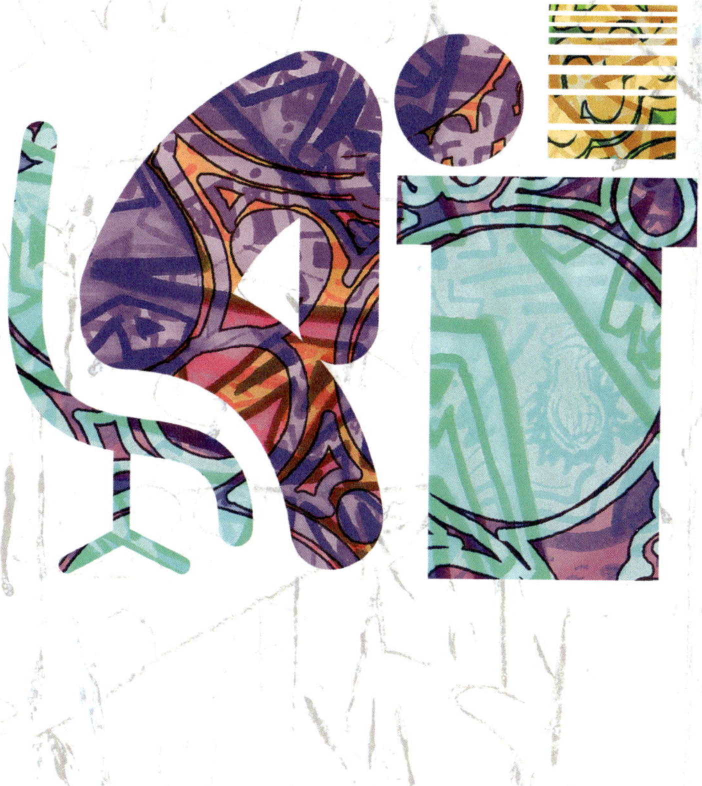

EVERYONE IN THE ROOM IS HAVING CONVERSATIONS, AND I'M STANDING HERE ALONE.
#ThisIsWhatAnxietyFeelsLike

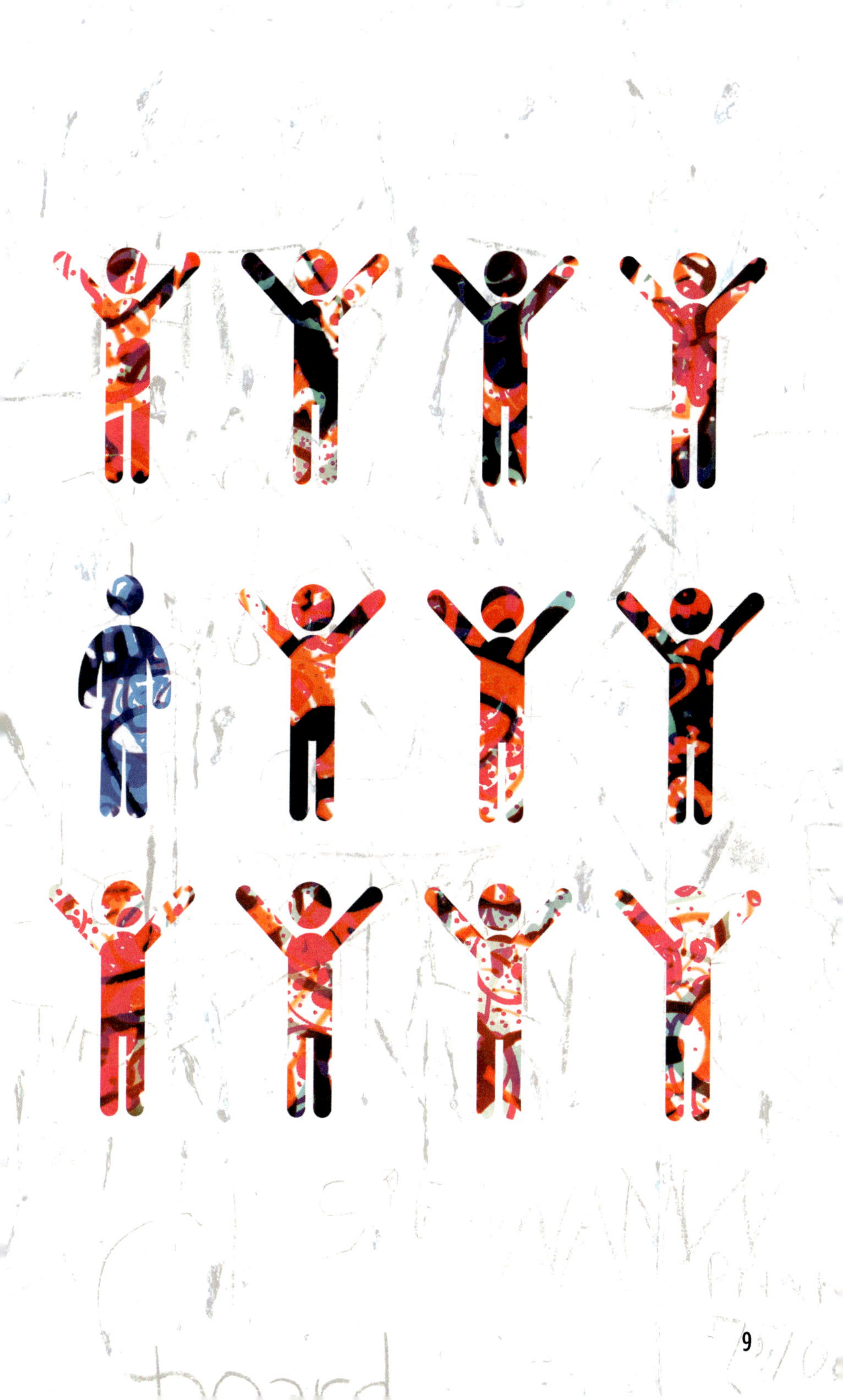

MY PRESCRIPTION IS ABOUT TO RUN OUT, AND I CAN'T GET IN TOUCH WITH MY PSYCHIATRIST.

#ThisIsWhatAnxietyFeelsLike

11

THE TRAIN IS BEING HELD BY THE DISPATCHER FOR 10 MINUTES NOW AND I DON'T KNOW WHAT'S GOING ON? AM I GOING TO DIE?

#ThisIsWhatAnxietyFeelsLike

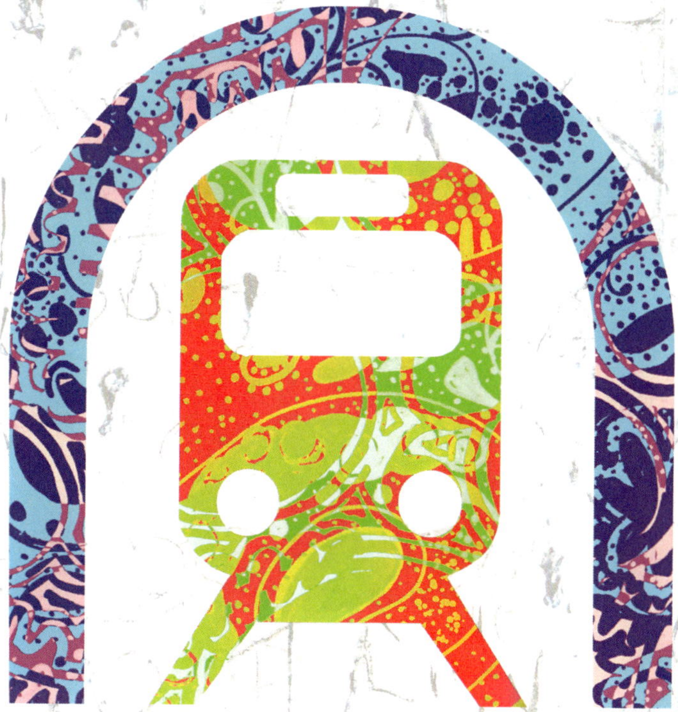

HR JUST CALLED ME AT MY DESK AND TOLD ME TO COME TO THEIR OFFICE
#ThisIsWhatAnxietyFeelsLike

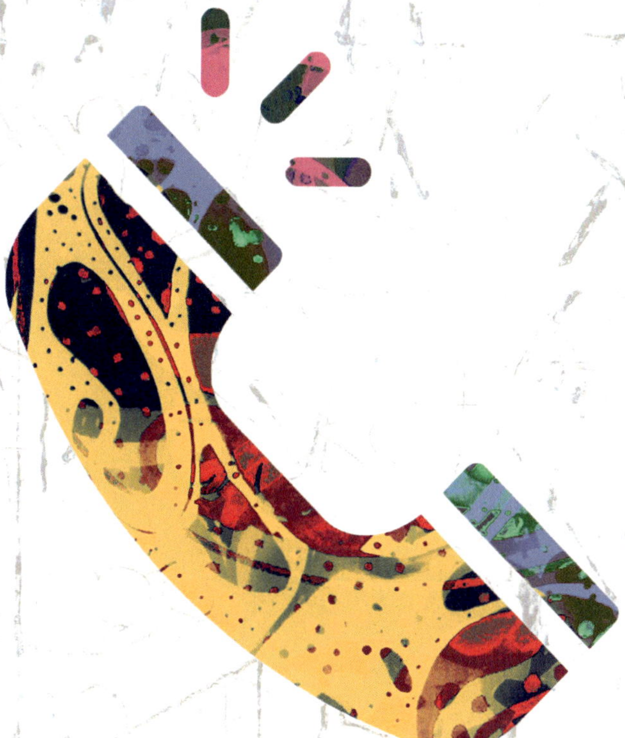

IS EVERYBODY STARING AT ME?
#ThisIsWhatAnxietyFeelsLike

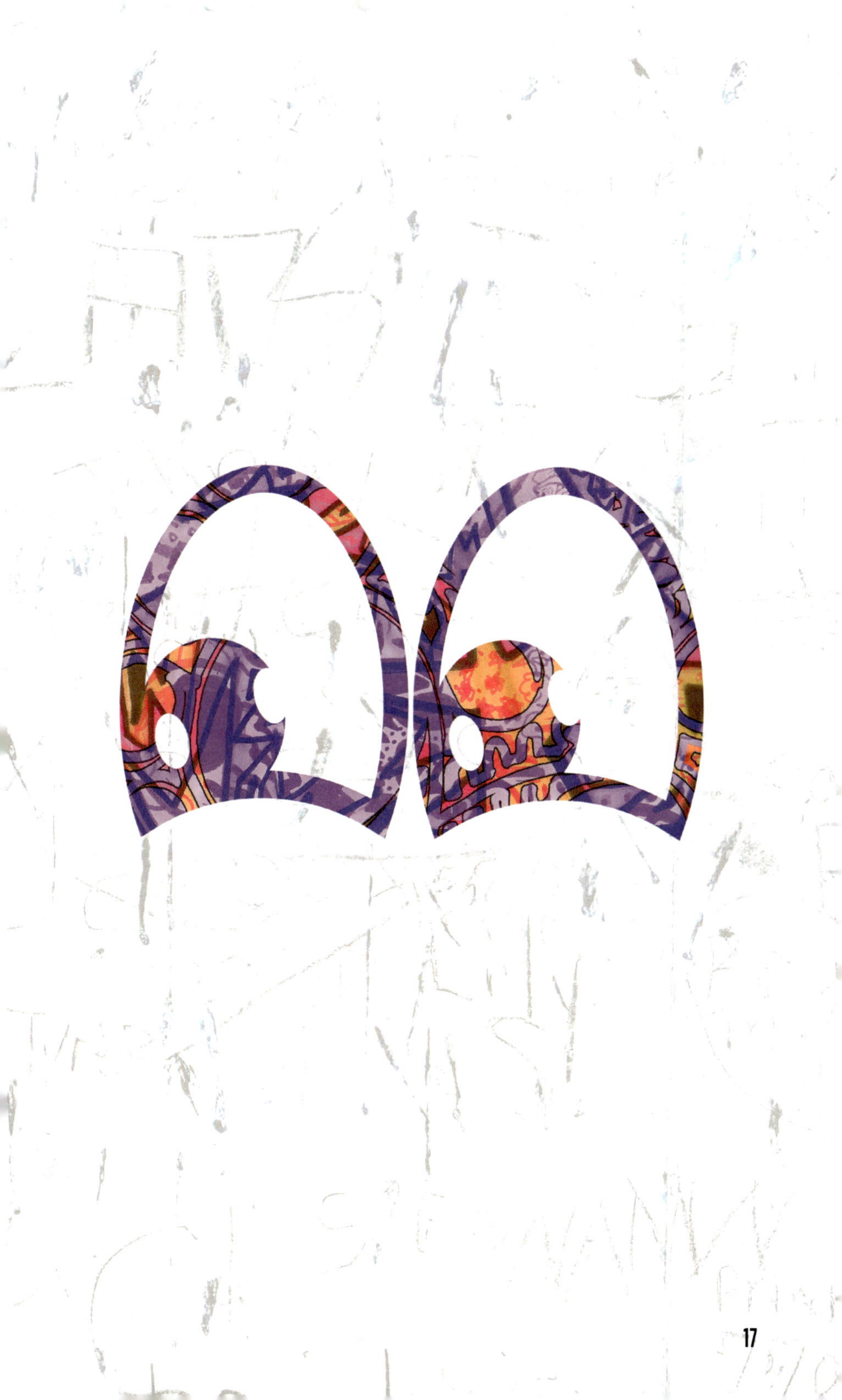

THE TAXIMETER IS GOING UP FASTER THAN I THOUGHT IT WOULD.
#ThisIsWhatAnxietyFeelsLike

19

WHAT'S HAPPENING WITH THE HEALTH CARE BILL?
#ThisIsWhatAnxietyFeelsLike

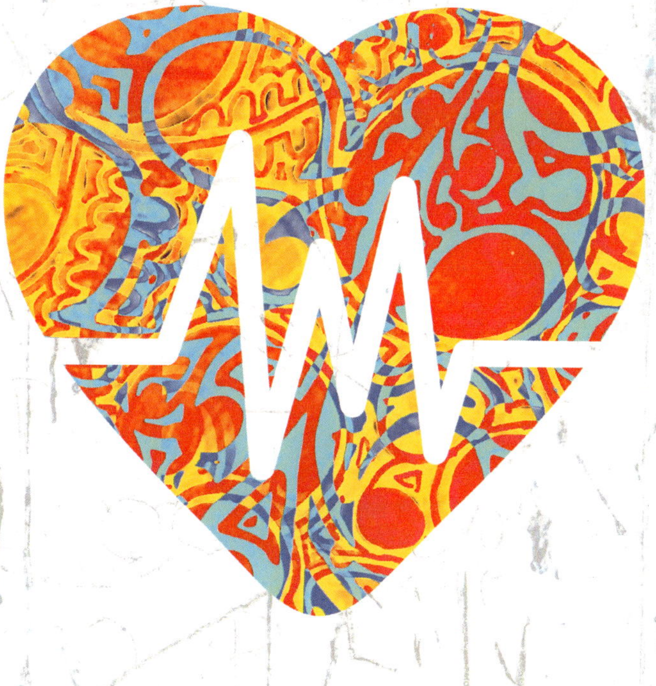

I'M GOING TO CHECK MY BANK BALANCE AND I AM TERRIFIED I'M OVERDRAWN.

#ThisIsWhatAnxietyFeelsLike

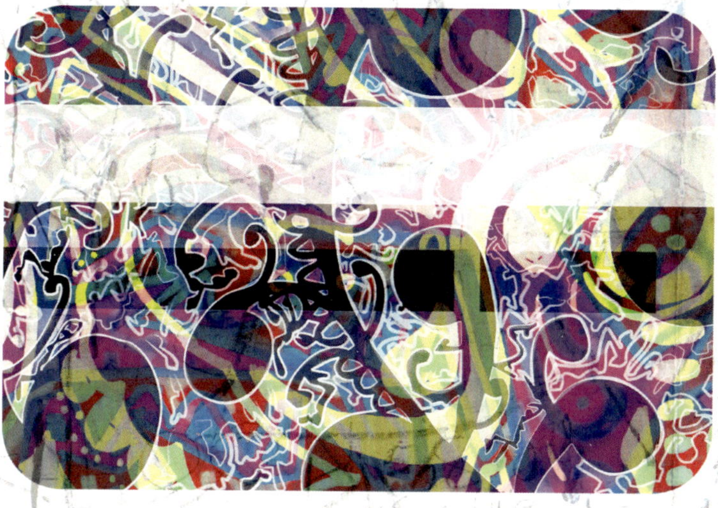

RENT IS DUE
#ThisIsWhatAnxietyFeelsLike

MY FRIEND HASN'T TEXTED ME BACK. HE HATES ME.
#ThisIsWhatAnxietyFeelsLike

I AM AFRAID OF DYING BECAUSE I HAVE A HEADACHE AND CLEARLY I HAVE A BRAIN TUMOR.

#ThisIsWhatAnxietyFeelsLike

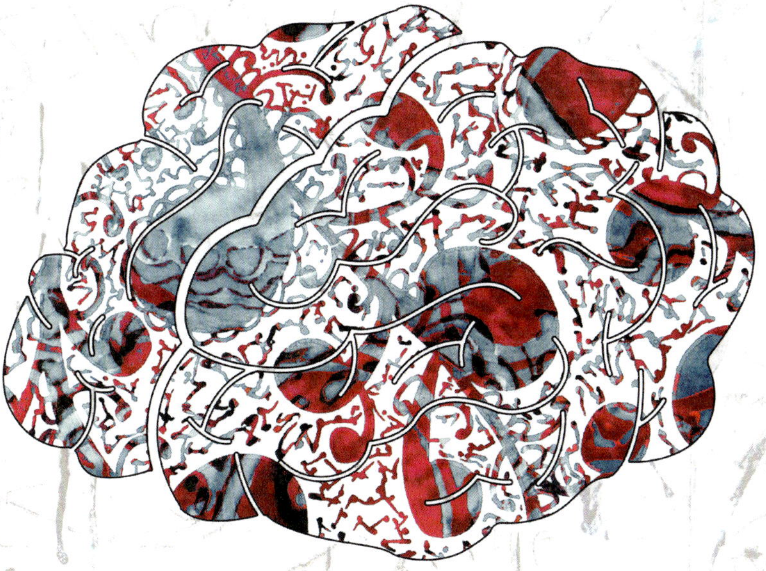

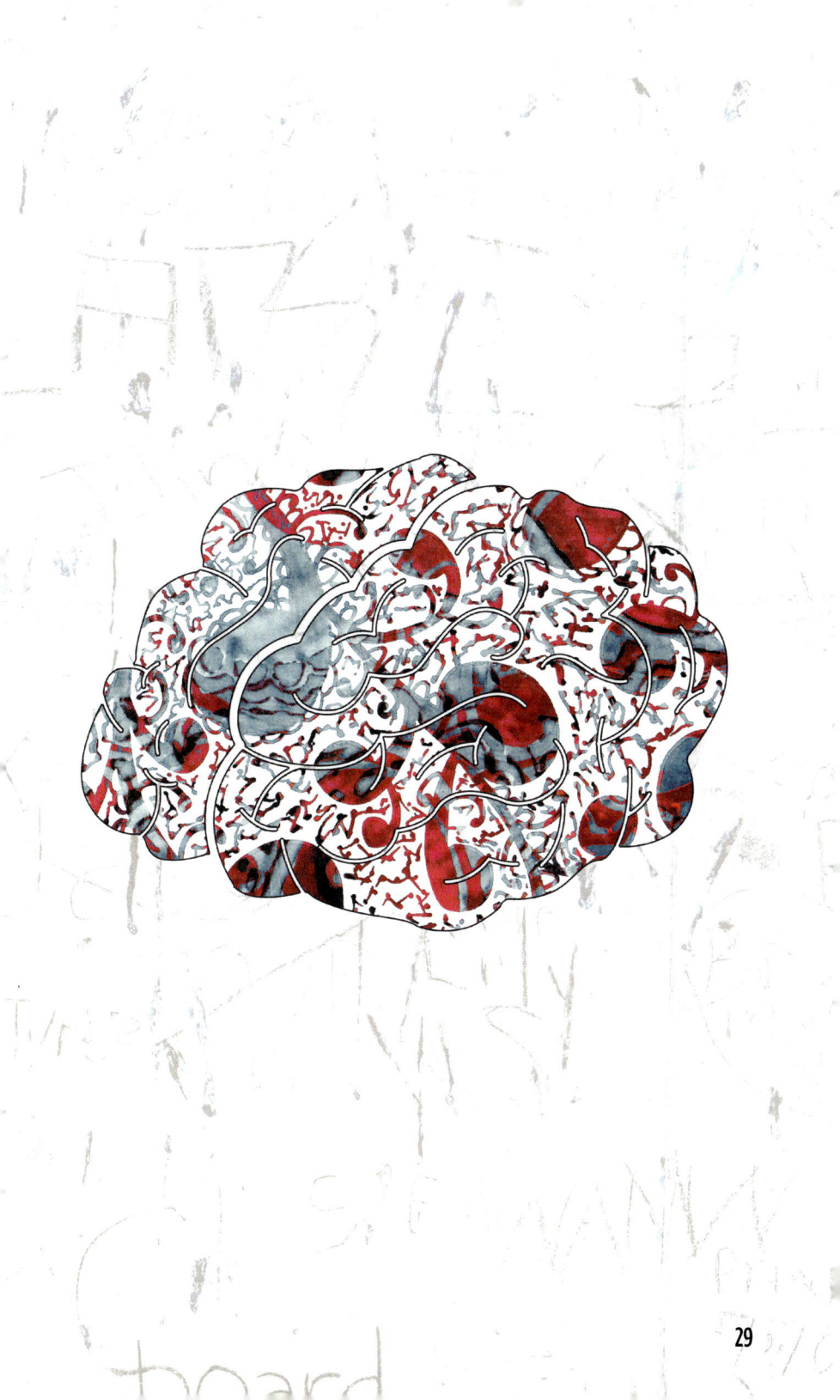

SOMETHING TERRIBLE IS GOING TO HAPPEN BECAUSE I THINK SOMETHING TERRIBLE IS GOING TO HAPPEN.

#ThisIsWhatAnxietyFeelsLike

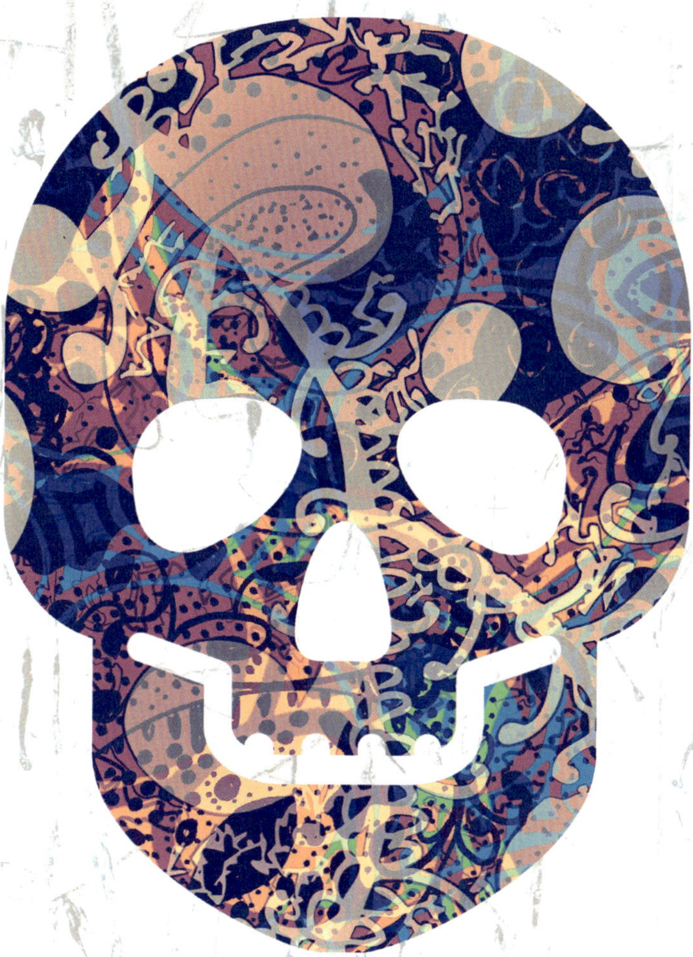

WHAT IF I CHOKE WHILE I'M ALONE?
#ThisIsWhatAnxietyFeelsLike

HELP

WHAT IF I NEVER FIND A BOYFRIEND OR GIRLFRIEND? I DON'T WANT TO DIE ALONE.
#ThisIsWhatAnxietyFeelsLike

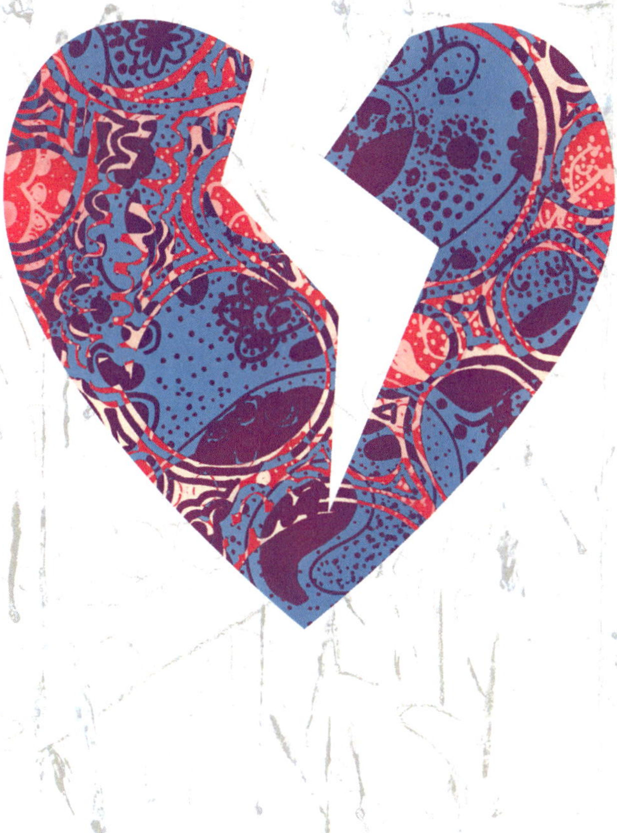

WHAT IF MY FRIENDS DON'T ACTUALLY WANT TO BE AROUND ME, AND I'M ANNOYING AND THEY'RE JUST TOLERATING ME TO BE NICE?

#ThisIsWhatAnxietyFeelsLike

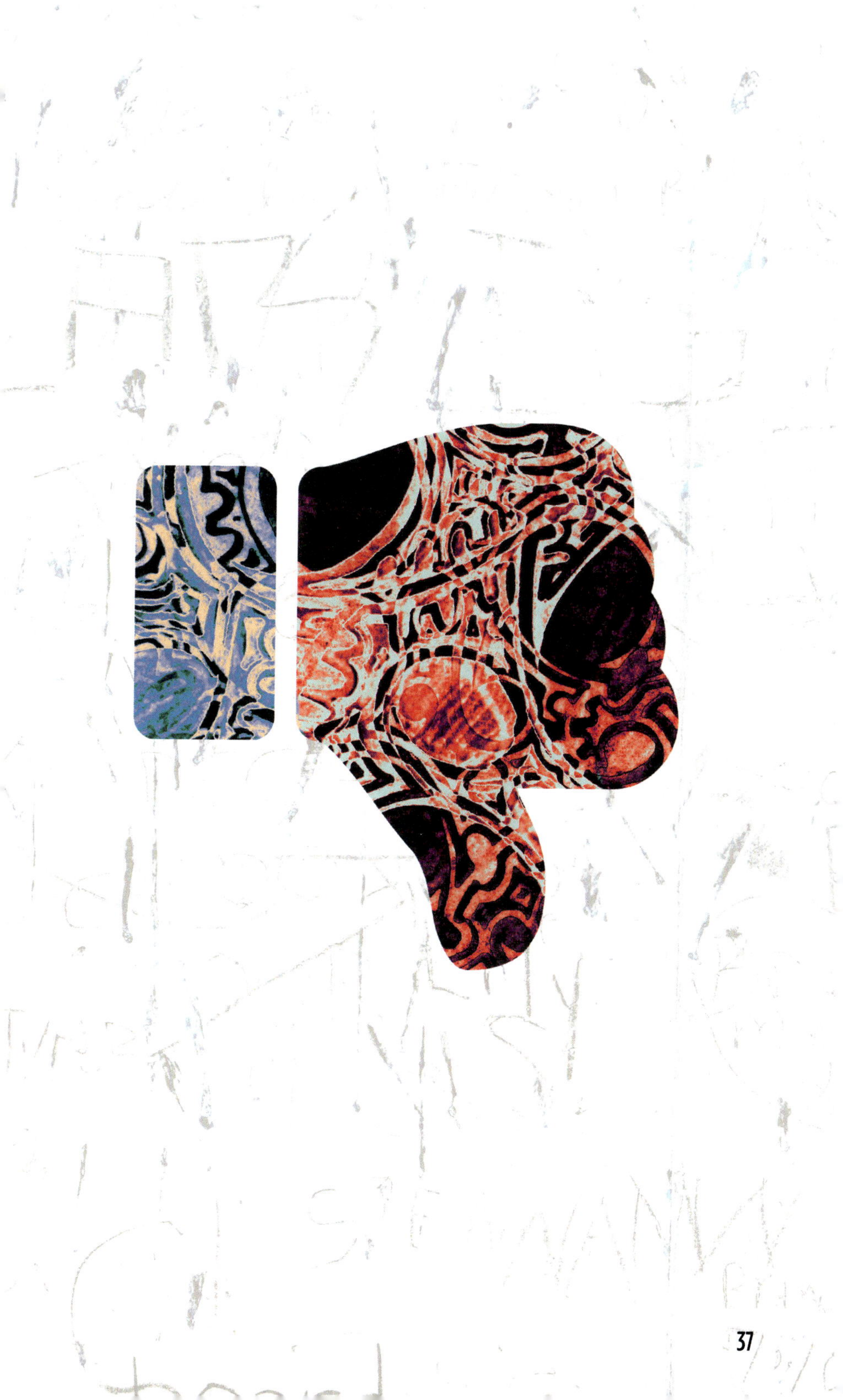

WHAT IF I DIE AND NOBODY FINDS ME FOR DAYS?

#ThisIsWhatAnxietyFeelsLike

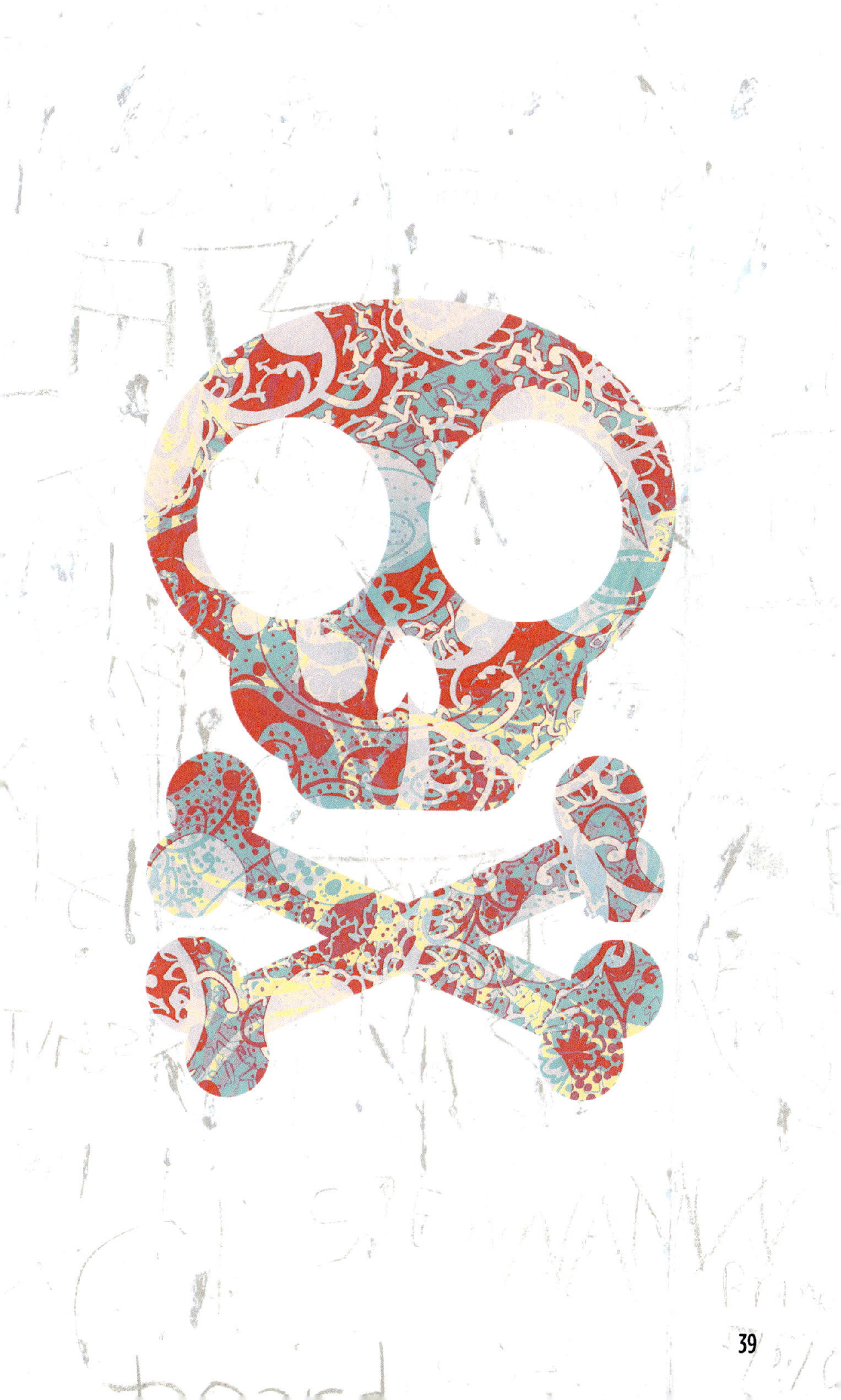

DO PEOPLE THINK I AM DRAMATIC OR EXAGGERATING? I'M HAVING A PANIC ATTACK.
#ThisIsWhatAnxietyFeelsLike

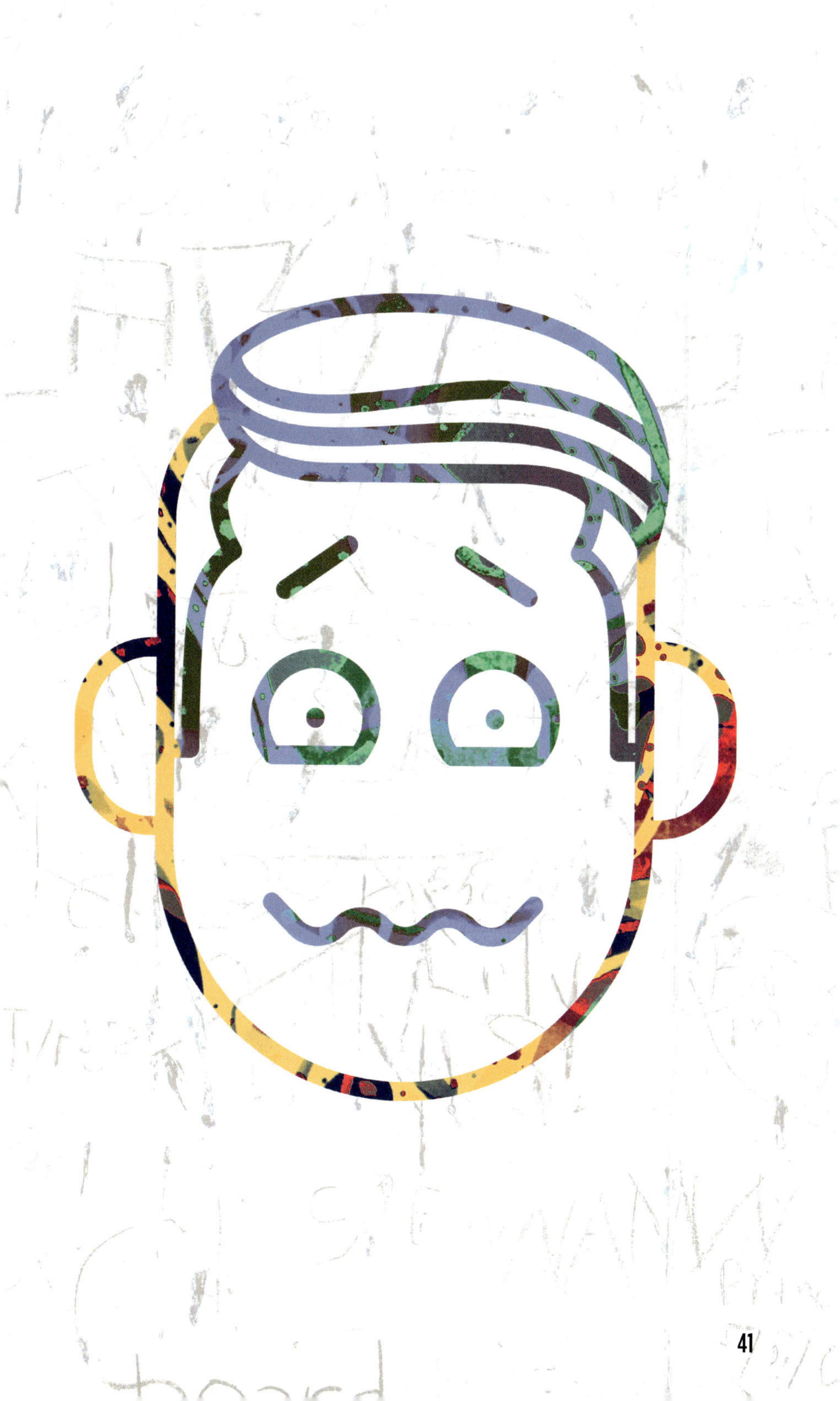

I'M AFRAID TO LEAVE THE HOUSE
#ThisIsWhatAnxietyFeelsLike

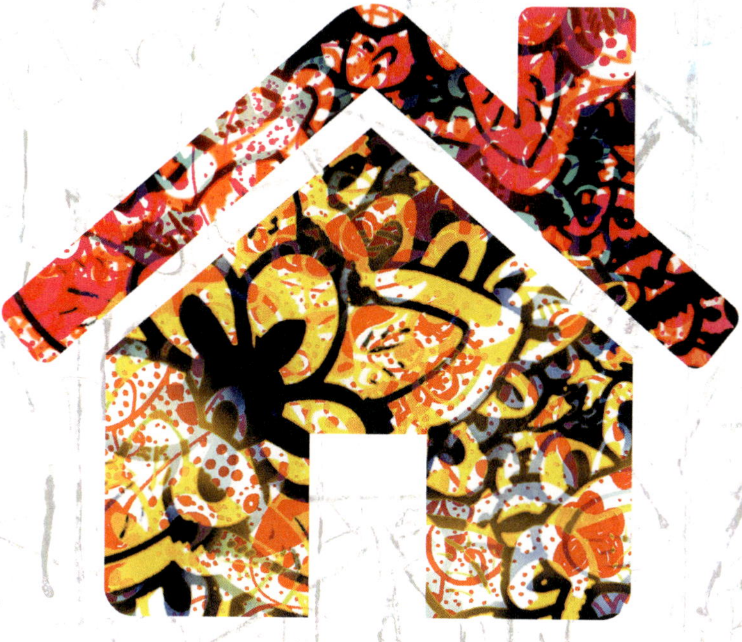

WHEN SOMEONE TELLS YOU TO "CALM DOWN" AND YOU CAN'T AND YOU FEEL EVEN WORSE ABOUT IT.

#ThisIsWhatAnxietyFeelsLike

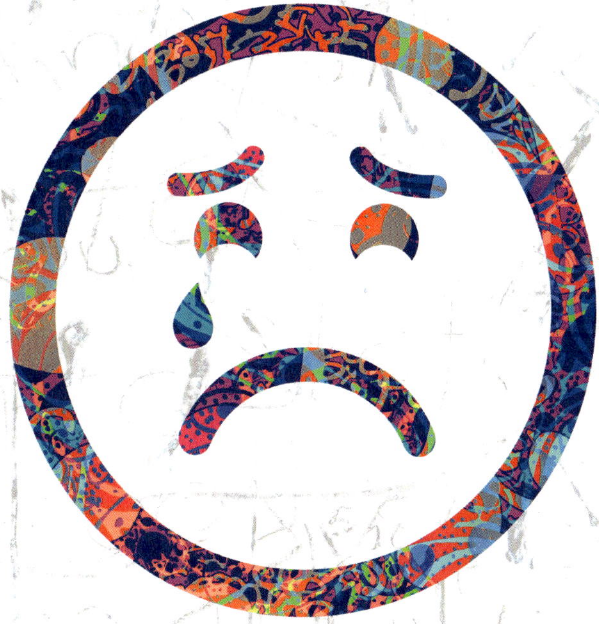

MY FRIEND HASN'T CALLED ME BACK. WHAT IF SOMETHING TERRIBLE HAPPENED TO HER?

#ThisIsWhatAnxietyFeelsLike

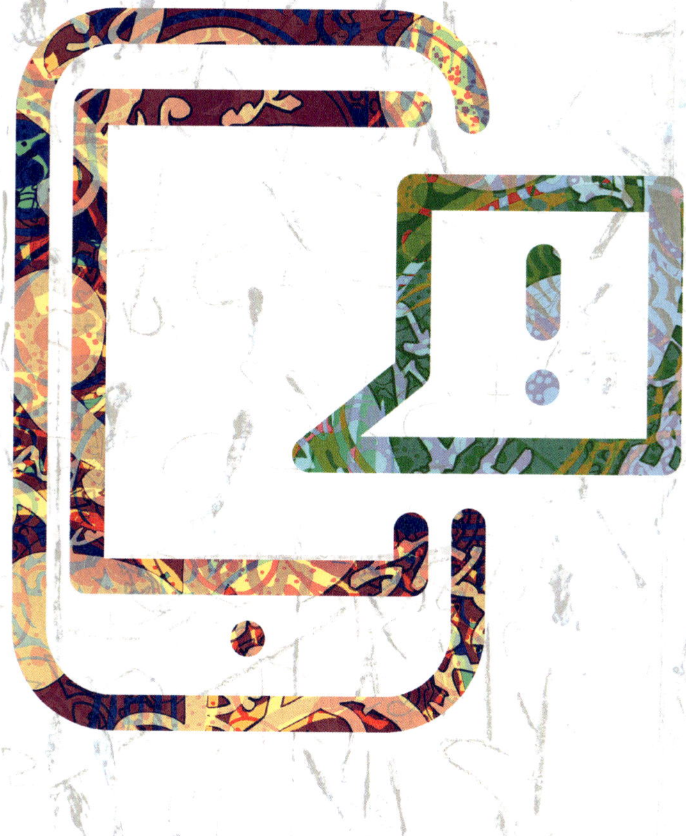

WHAT IF I HAVE A DISEASE BECAUSE I LOOKED IT UP ONLINE?

#ThisIsWhatAnxietyFeelsLike

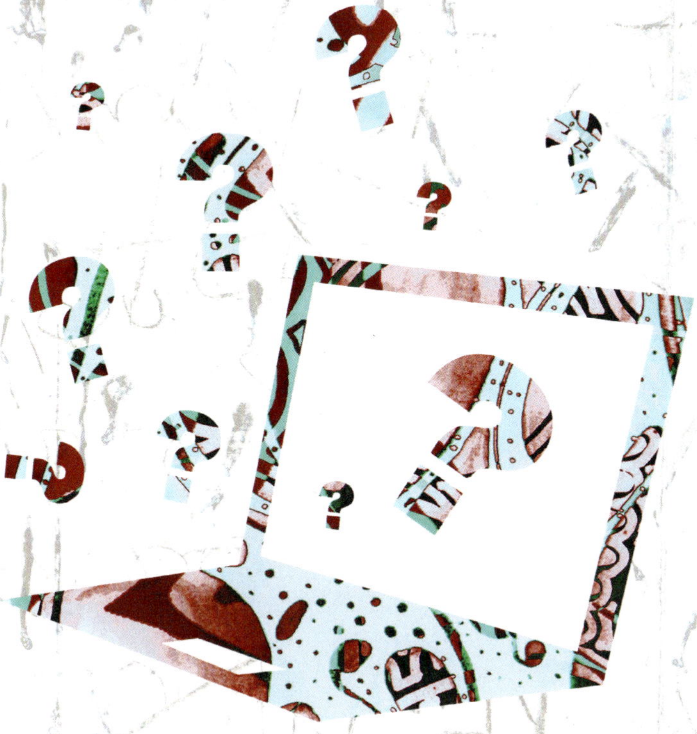

I THINK PEOPLE KNOW MY DEEP DARKEST SECRETS
#ThisIsWhatAnxietyFeelsLike

I'M HIDING FROM PEOPLE AT A PARTY RIGHT NOW

#ThisIsWhatAnxietyFeelsLike

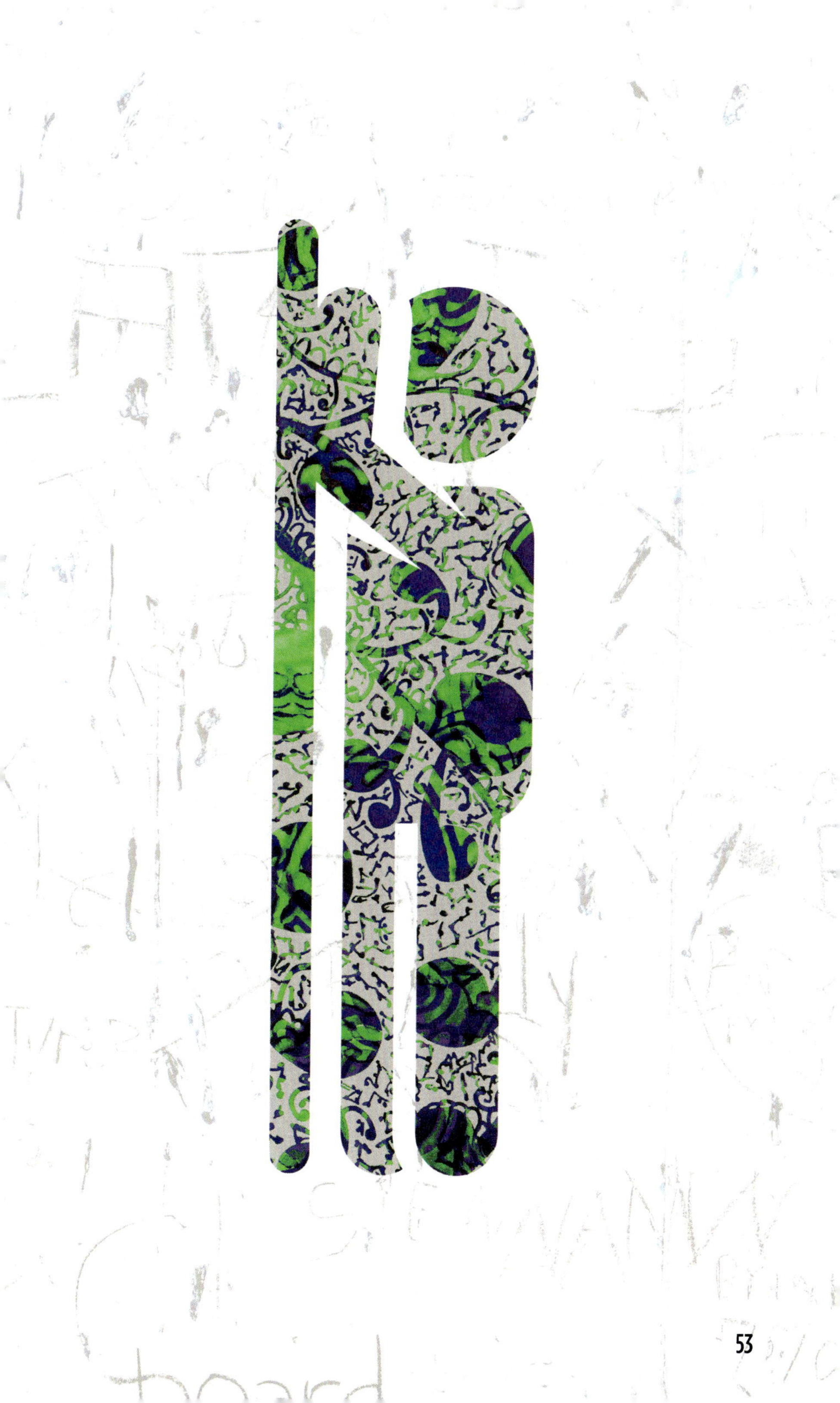

ARE PEOPLE ARE LAUGHING AT ME?
#ThisIsWhatAnxietyFeelsLike

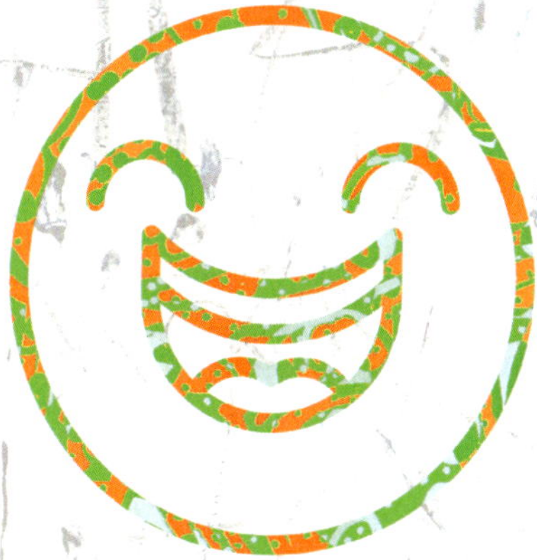

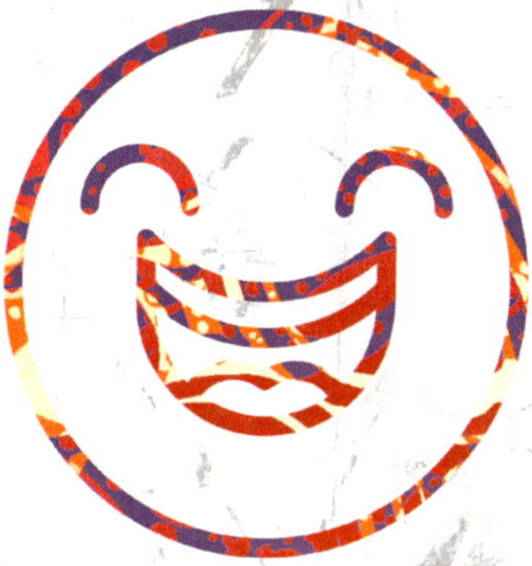

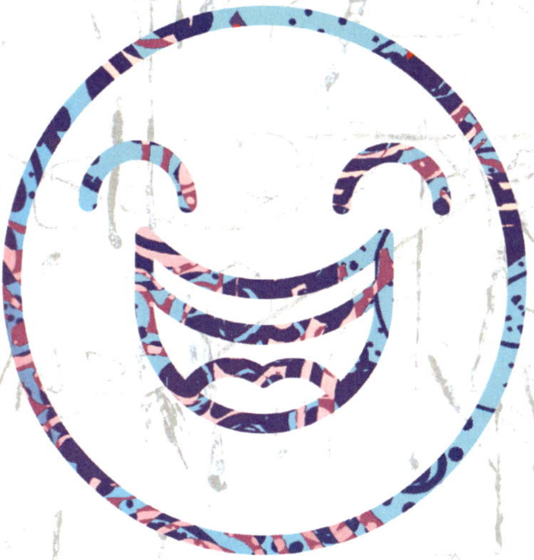

I JUST WOKE UP AND I'M SWEATING, MY HEART IS RACING, AND I FEEL LIKE I'M GOING TO DIE

#ThisIsWhatAnxietyFeelsLike

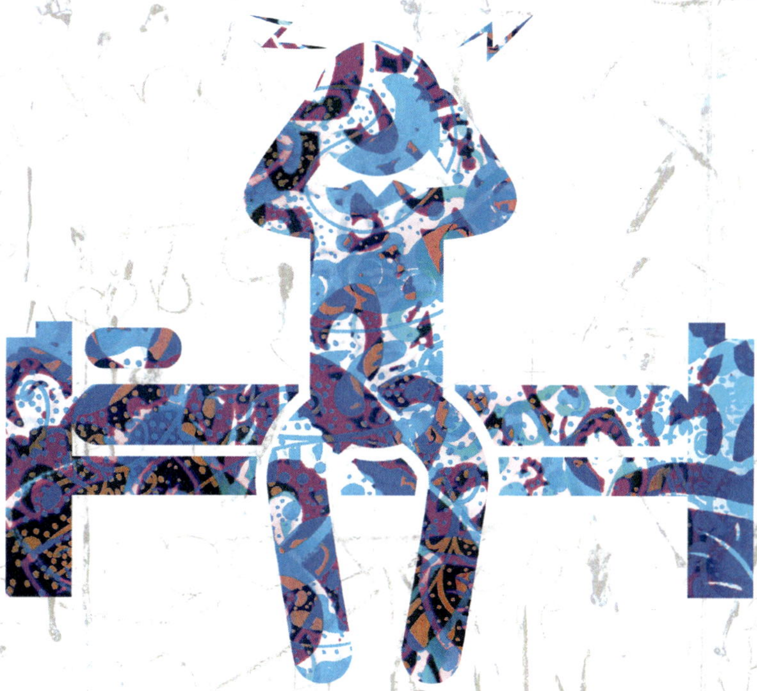

I THINK I'M BEING IGNORED BY EVERYBODY
#ThisIsWhatAnxietyFeelsLike

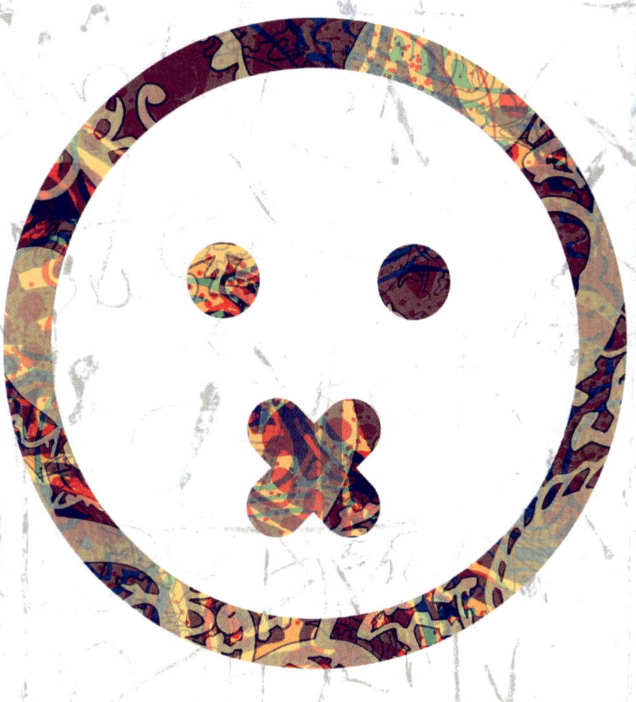

I AM NEVER GOING TO BE OKAY AGAIN

#ThisIsWhatAnxietyFeelsLike

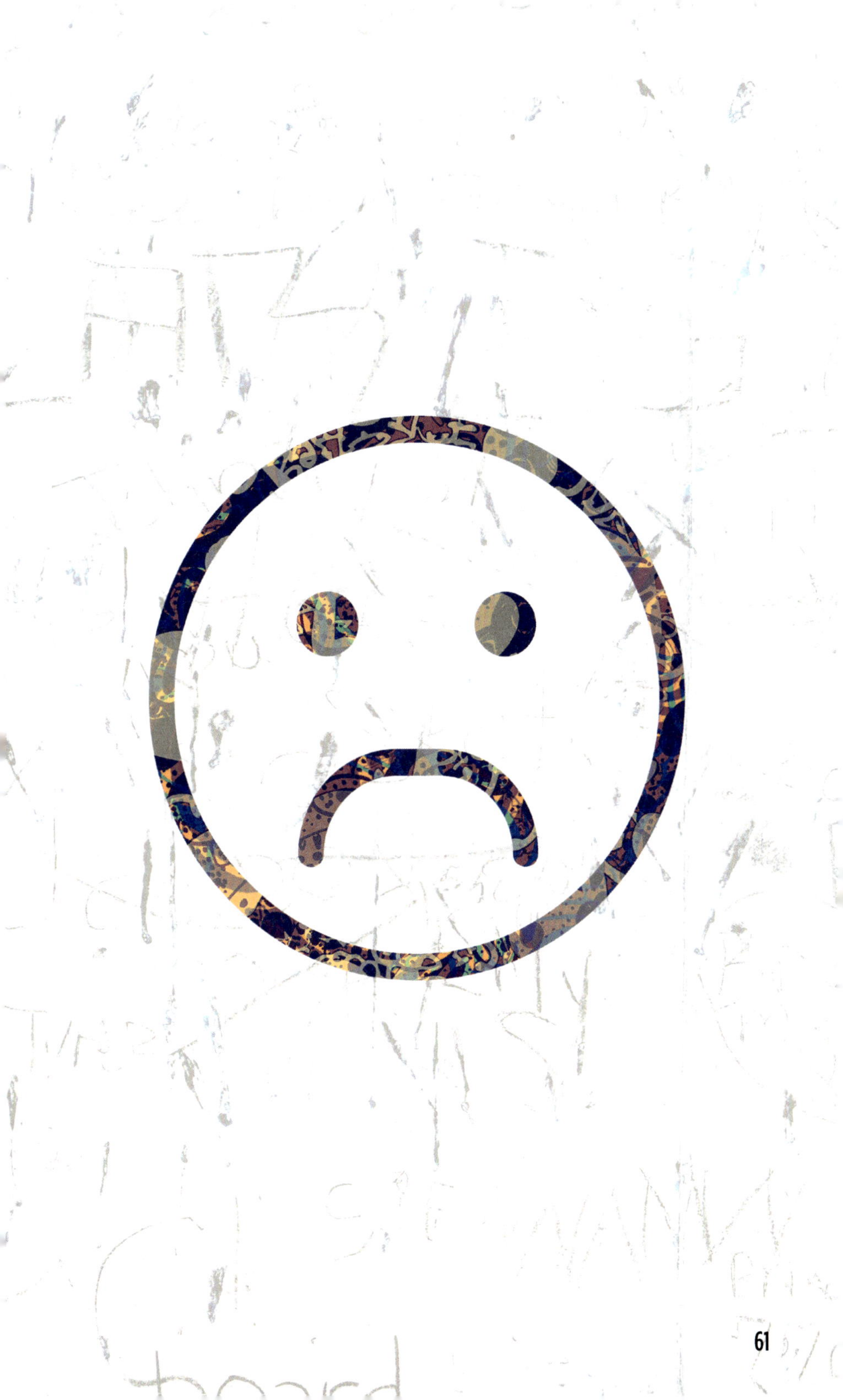

I CANT FIGURE OUT WHAT I'M FEELING BECAUSE THERE ARE TOO MANY FEELINGS.

#ThisIsWhatAnxietyFeelsLike

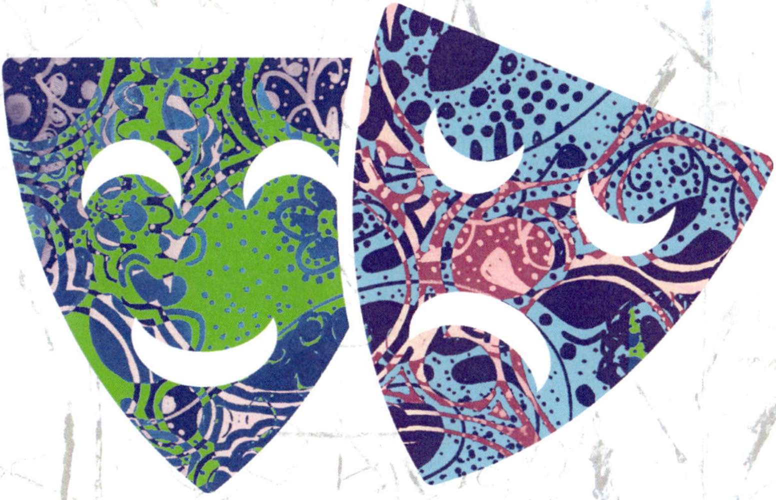

THERE'S AN ELEPHANT ON MY CHEST AND I CAN'T BREATHE.
#ThisIsWhatAnxietyFeelsLike

65

I FEEL OVEREXPOSED.
#ThisIsWhatAnxietyFeelsLike

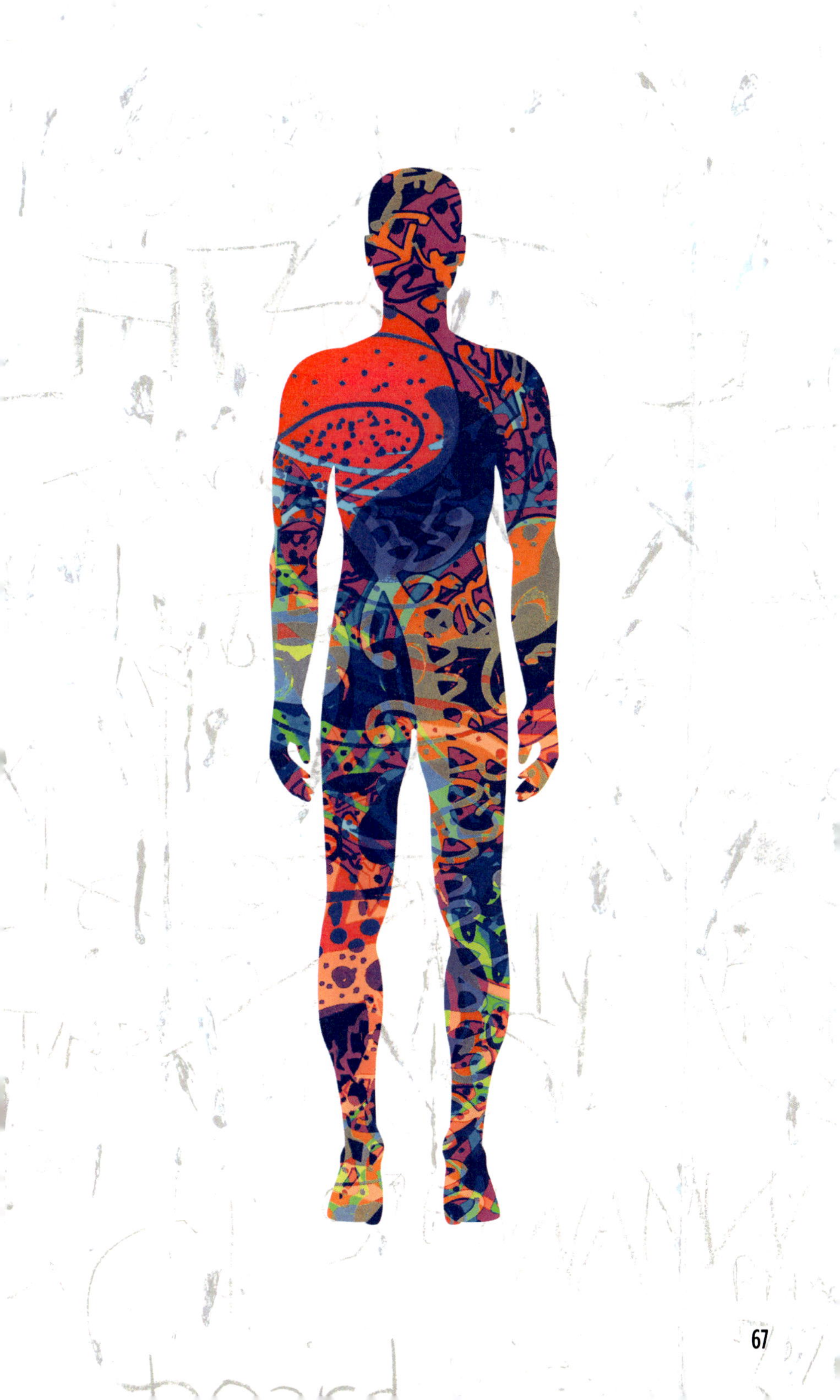

PEOPLE HATE WHAT I AM WEARING
#ThisIsWhatAnxietyFeelsLike

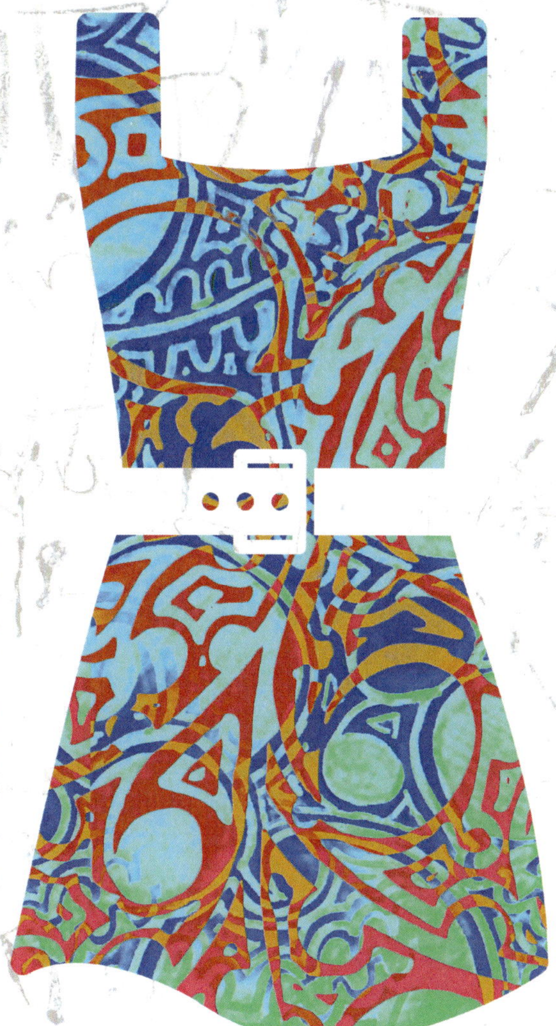

I NEED TO DO THIS RIGHT NOW.
#ThisIsWhatAnxietyFeelsLike

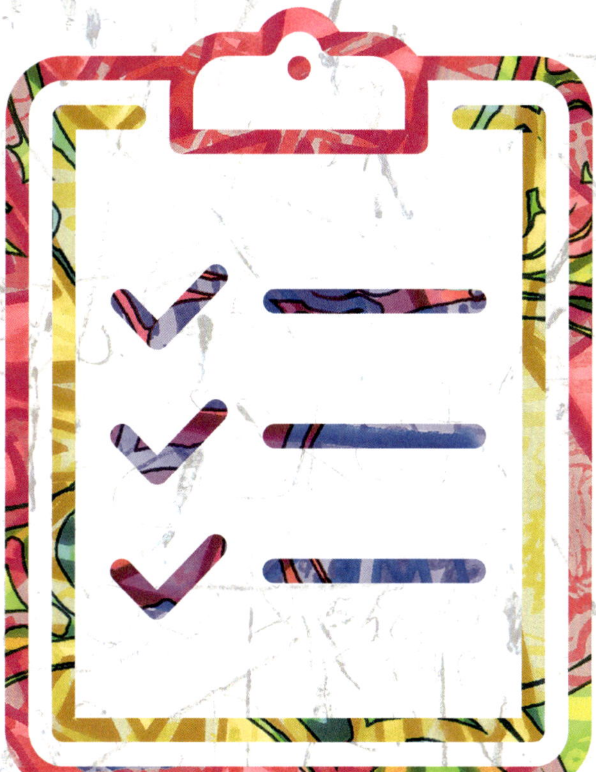

I DON'T WANT TO GO ANYWHERE OR TALK TO ANYONE.
#ThisIsWhatAnxietyFeelsLike

73

NOBODY UNDERSTANDS ME.
#ThisIsWhatAnxietyFeelsLike

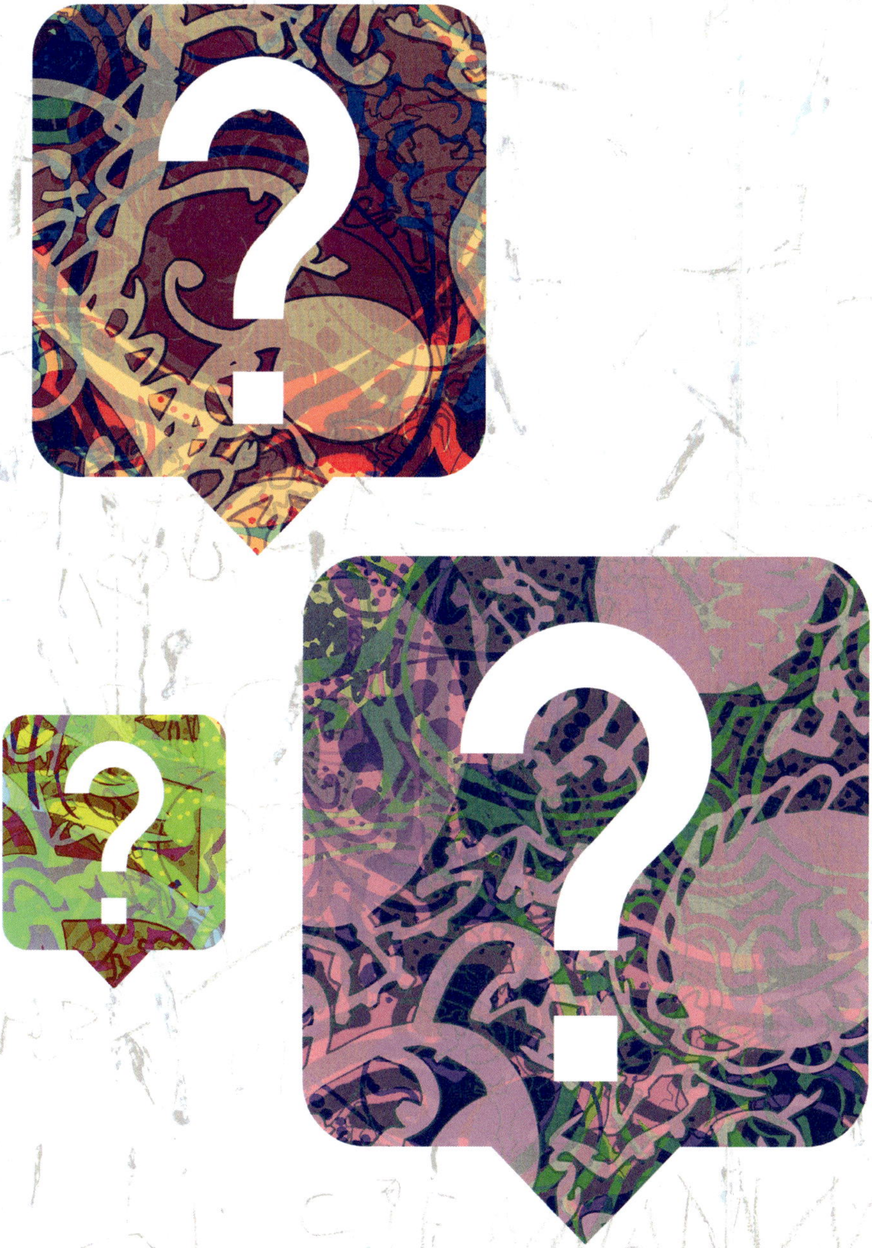

MY BRAIN DOESN'T SHUT UP.
#ThisIsWhatAnxietyFeelsLike

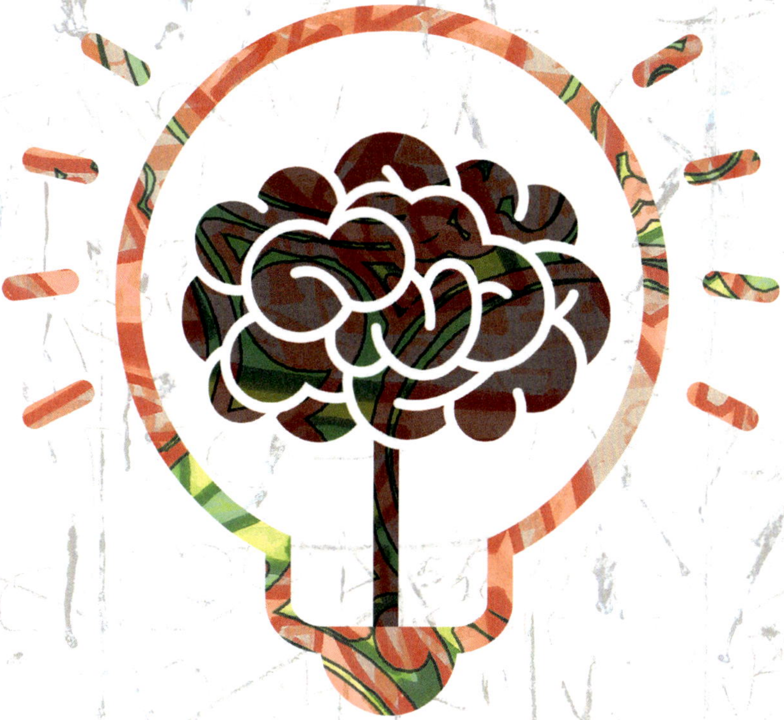

I'M OBSESSING OVER MY EX, EVEN THOUGH THEY'VE MOVED ON.

#ThisIsWhatAnxietyFeelsLike

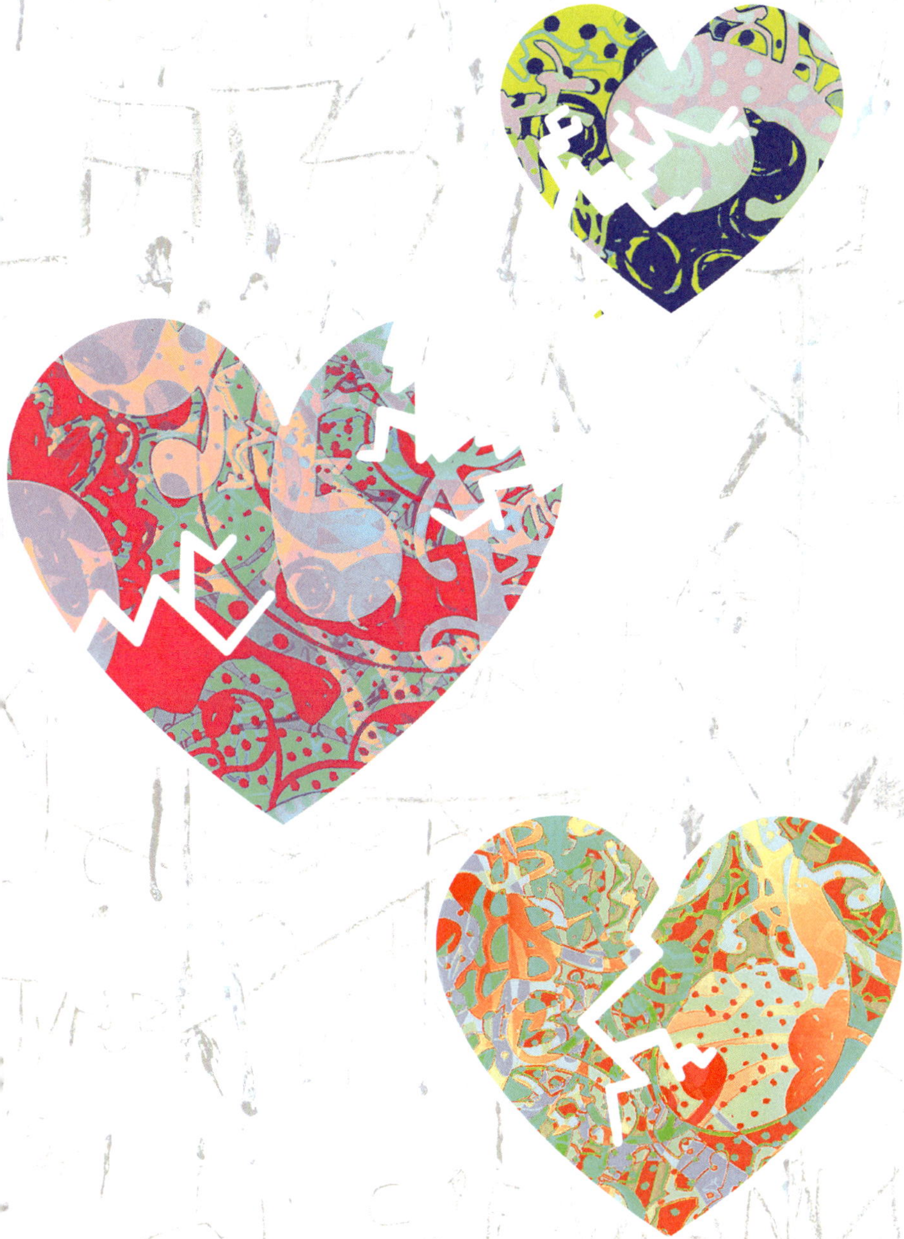

WHATS GOING TO HAPPEN IN THE FUTURE?
#ThisIsWhatAnxietyFeelsLike

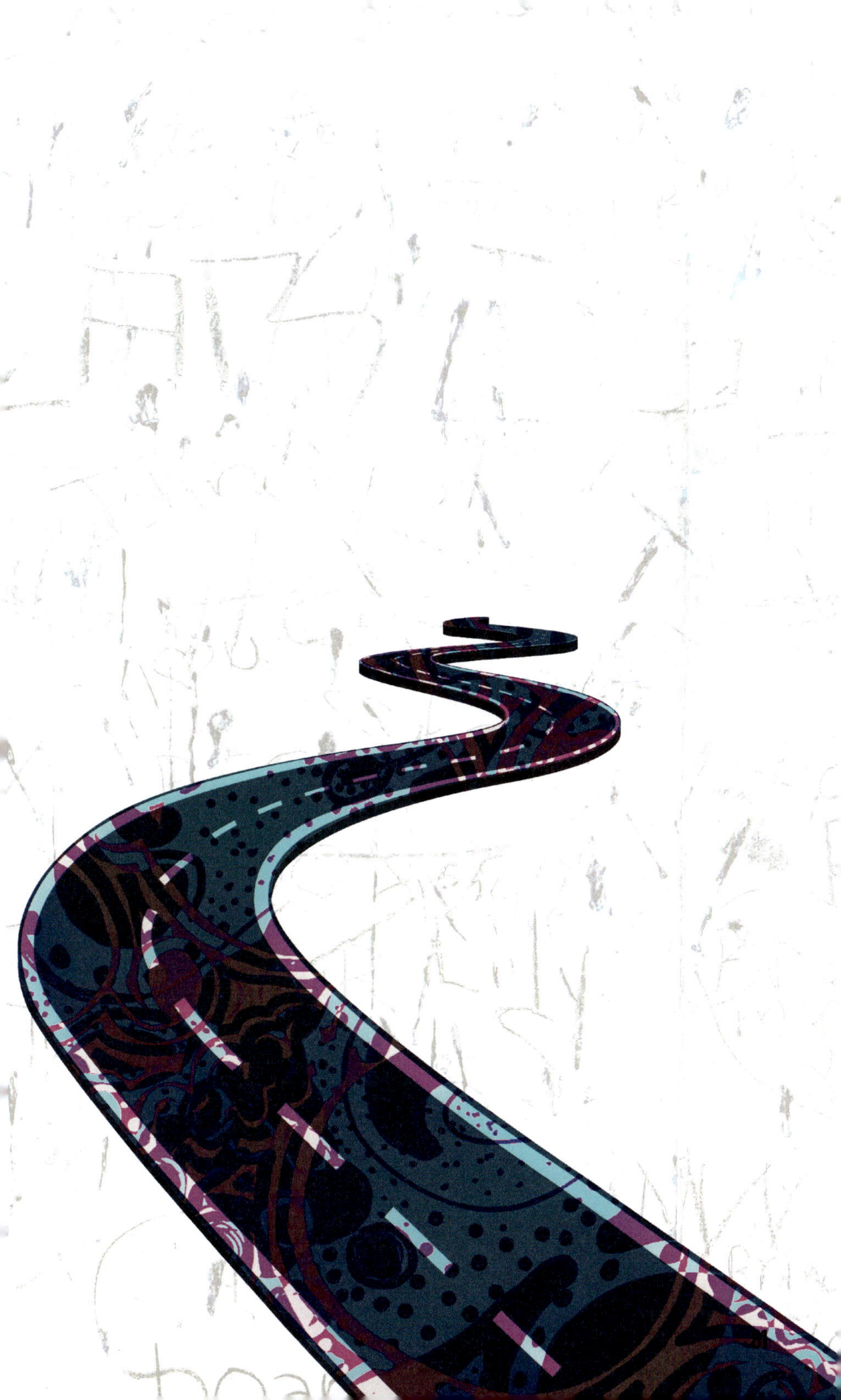

I'M SO WORRIED I CAN'T EAT ANYTHING

#ThisIsWhatAnxietyFeelsLike

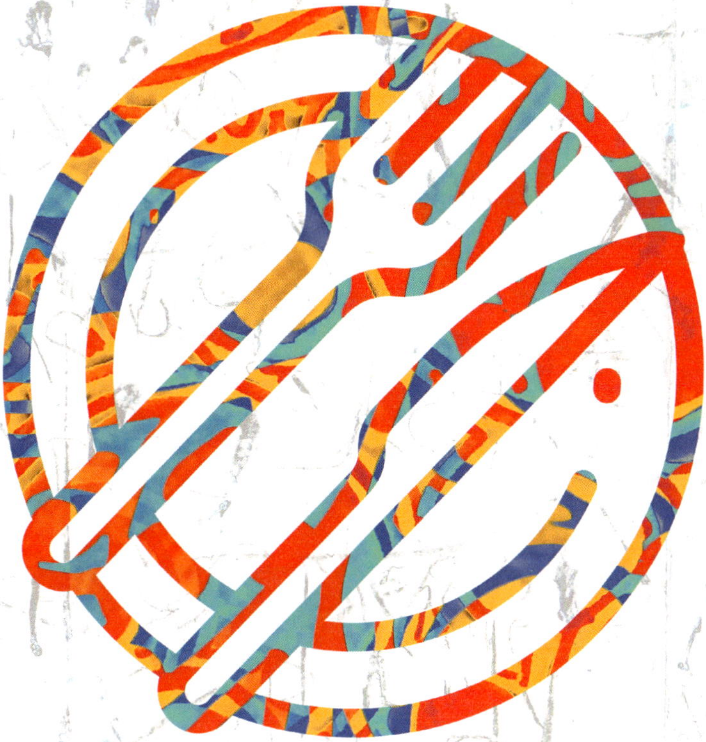

I THINK BEING INSIDE OVERWHELMS MY BRAIN
#ThisIsWhatAnxietyFeelsLike

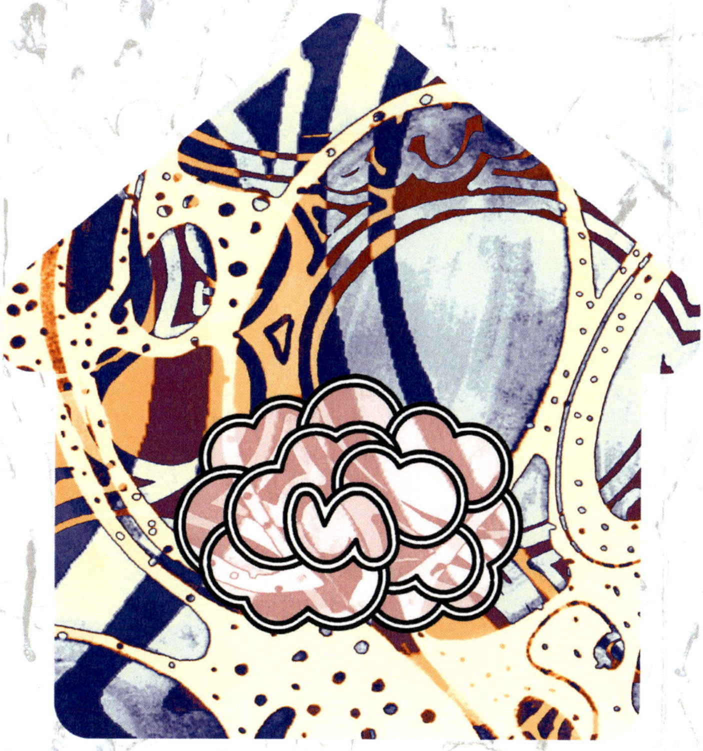

I CAN'T SLEEP...EVER.
#ThisIsWhatAnxietyFeelsLike

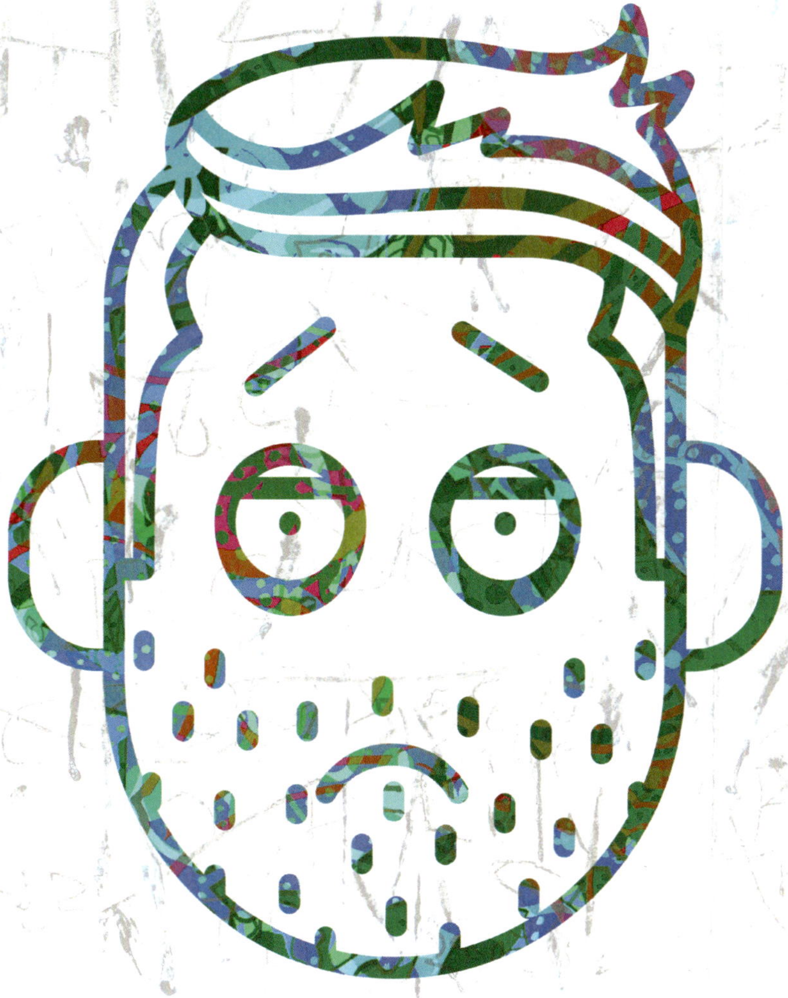

I'M AFRAID OF EVERYTHING.
#ThisIsWhatAnxietyFeelsLike

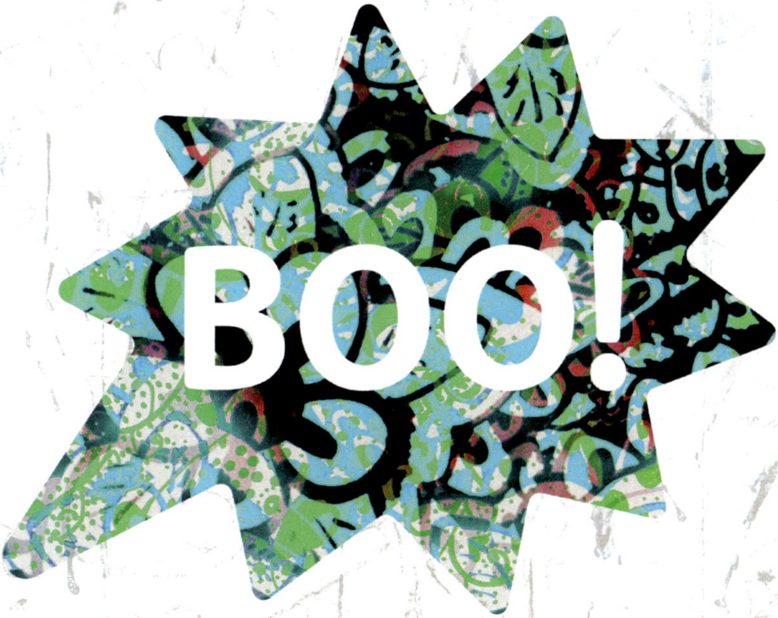
BOO!

SOMETHING TERRIBLE IS GOING TO HAPPEN.
#ThisIsWhatAnxietyFeelsLike

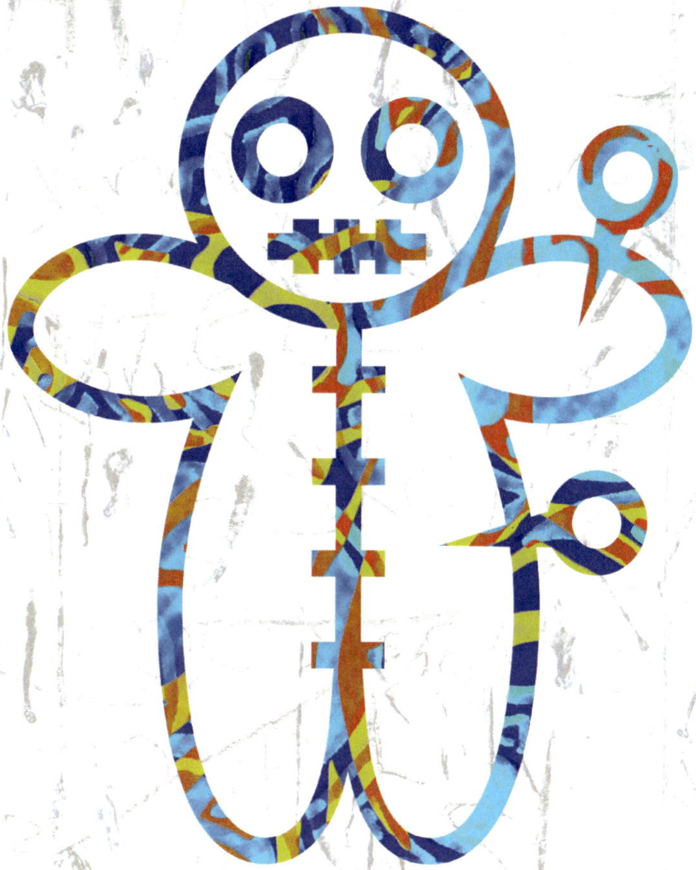

I'M REPLAYING ALL THE CONVERSATIONS I'VE HAD TODAY.

#ThisIsWhatAnxietyFeelsLike

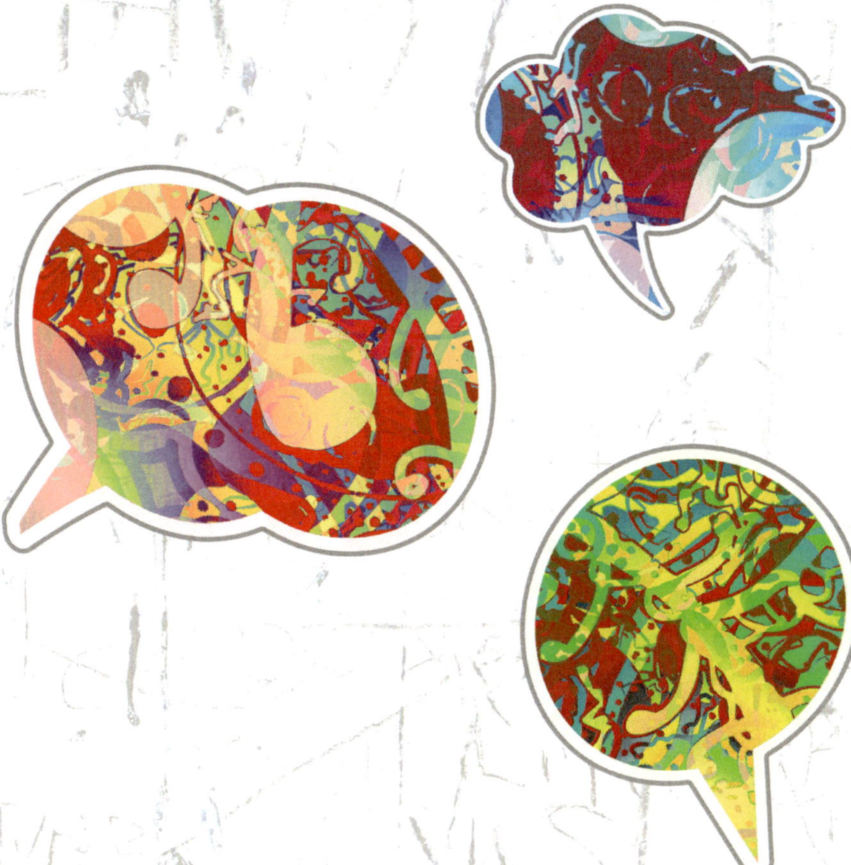

WANT TO FIX THINGS THAT I HAVE NO CONTROL OVER.
#ThisIsWhatAnxietyFeelsLike

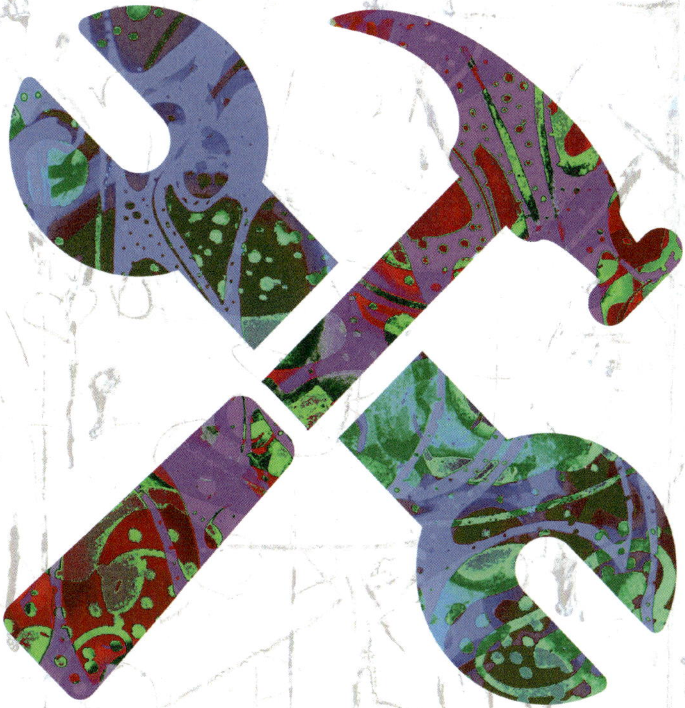

DID I JUST OFFEND SOMEONE?
#ThisIsWhatAnxietyFeelsLike

!@%&*#

I'M WORRIED I BOTHER MY FRIENDS WHEN I CALL.
#ThisIsWhatAnxietyFeelsLike

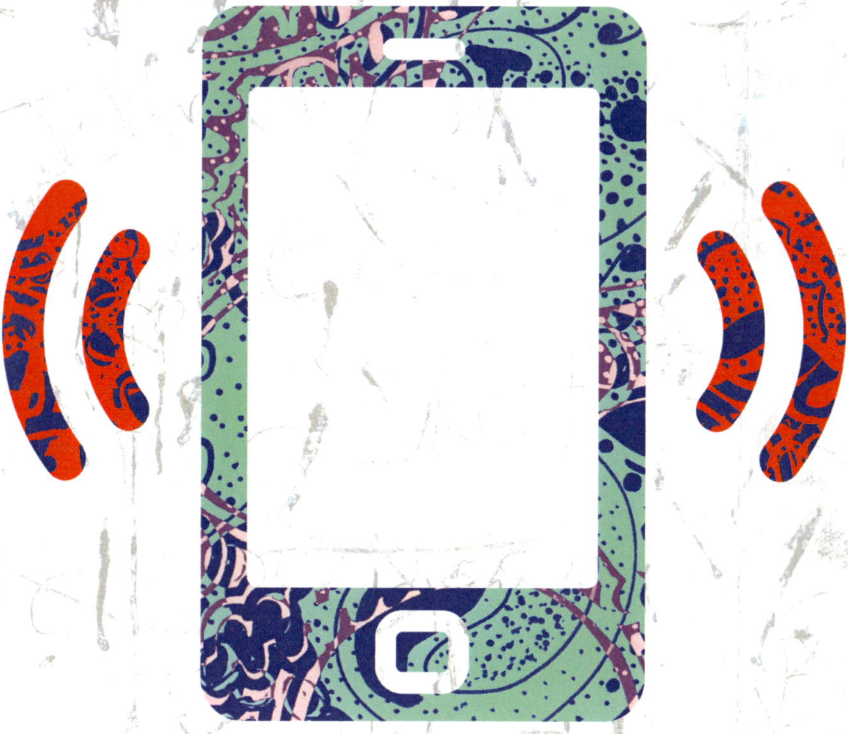

I CONSTANTLY APOLOGIZE TO PEOPLE.
#ThisIsWhatAnxietyFeelsLike

101

WHY WON'T MY THERAPIST ANSWER MY CALL?

#ThisIsWhatAnxietyFeelsLike

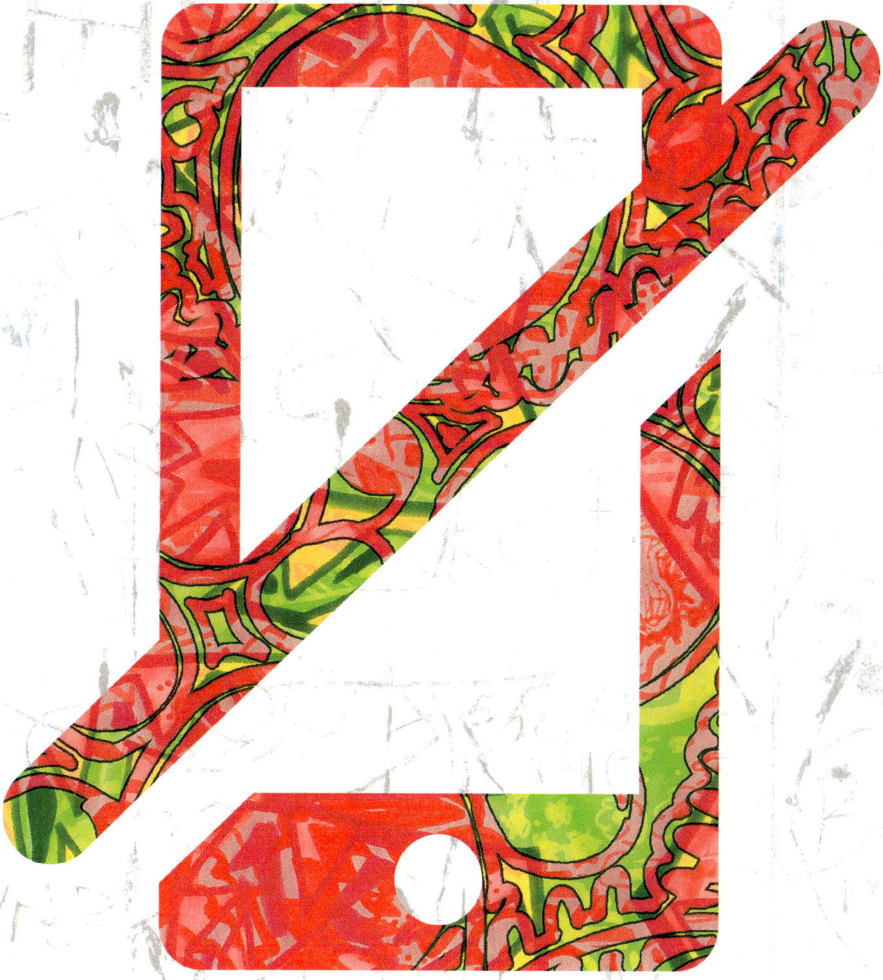

WHAT IF SOMEONE SEES ME TAKE MY MEDS?

#ThisIsWhatAnxietyFeelsLike

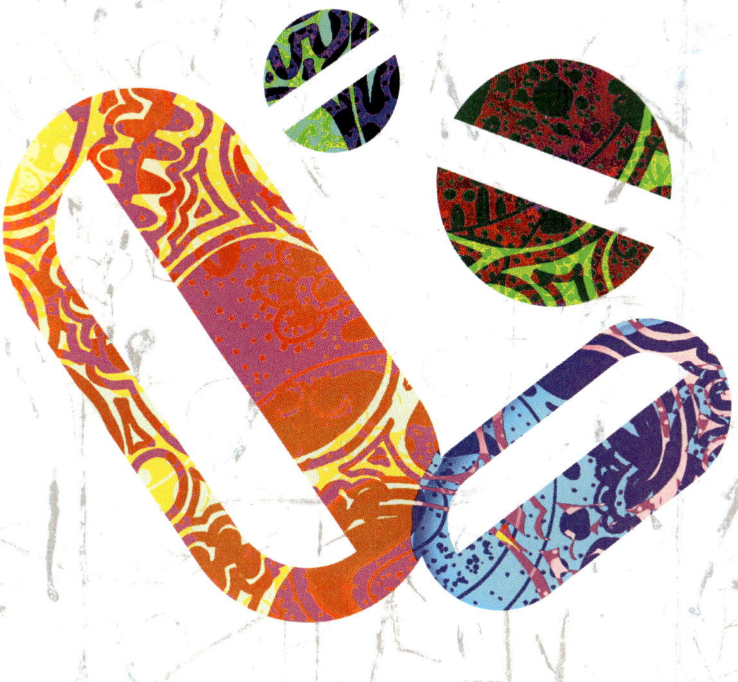

WHAT IF I MADE AN ERROR DESIGNING THIS BOOK?

#ThisIsWhatAnxietyFeelsLike

#THIS IS WHAT ANXIETY FEELS LIKE

WHEN YOU THINK EVERYONE HATES YOU & SO MUCH MORE

SARAH FADER
MICHELLE HAMMER

Made in the USA
Middletown, DE
21 August 2018